ON SOUTHERN METALS

Plate 1: A 'Schools' class 4-4-0 locomotive, No. 30911 *Dover* is seen at Eastleigh Shed on 8th August 1959, being prepared to work a boat train from Southampton Docks. This particular engine worked the last Central Section steam working on 28th December 1962, before being withdrawn the next day.

Plate 2: North of Winchester on a sunny 16th July 1960, 'King Arthur' class 4-6-0, No. 30782 *Sir Brian* heads a Bournemouth to Waterloo train. Being formed of all Maunsell corridor stock, this train is typical of a pre-1939 Southern express.

Copyright © 1984 Oxford Publishing Co.

ISBN 0-86093-215-X

Typesetting by:
Aquarius Typesetting Services, New Milton, Hants.

Printed in Great Britain by:
Wm. Clowes Ltd., Beccles.

Published by:
Oxford Publishing Co.
Link House
West Street
POOLE, Dorset

ON SOUTHERN METALS

Les Elsey

Oxford Publishing Company

Introduction

This book is a pictorial record of the various types of motive power which worked on the Southern Region between 1950 and 1967, when steam was finally ended with the Bournemouth line electrification. There has been no attempt to portray only Southern Railway motive power in this album or even show steam only, but a cross-section of BR motive power which worked over the region in the eighteen years is featured.

In 1950, Bulleid was still in command, and Pacifics were still being built at Eastleigh and Brighton. Also the first and only 'Leader' class locomotive was completed and ran trials. The year 1952 brought the 'Britannia' class to the Southern Region, when these engines were loaned for evaluation, and the Festival of Britain exhibit, No. 70004 *William Shakespeare*, became the pride of Stewarts Lane Shed, being used for working the 'Golden Arrow' boat train. In 1953, a Pacific broke a driving axle at Crewkerne whilst at speed but luckily, no injuries were caused. This is turn effected the temporary withdrawal of the whole of the Bulleid Pacifics for ultrasonic axle testing. The Southern Region borrowed locomotives from other regions, with Classes V2, and V1, Standard Class 5s, LMS 'Black Fives', and 'Britannias' covering this withdrawal which lasted for about two months. From then on, the Southern Railway classes were gradually being withdrawn as new Standard classes were introduced. The first Bulleid 'Merchant Navy' rebuilds were introduced in 1956 which, in the opinion of the author, gave them the appearance of 'real' engines. This in turn brought the rebuilding, in 1957, of the smaller Pacifics, which culminated in thirty 'Merchant Navy' and sixty 'West Country' and 'Battle of Britain' class locomotives being converted. On the diesel side, the appearance of the three Southern Region main line locomotives between 1951 and 1954 was followed by the loan of the two 1947 built LMS diesels which worked on quite arduous schedules until they were all sent to the London Midland Region in 1955. In the meantime, the diesel shunter was beginning to make its mark in the Southern Region's marshalling yards commencing in Norwood and Hither Green in 1951, resulting in the ultimate withdrawal of some of the various steam shunters. Diesel electric multiple units were introduced on the Hastings line and to the Hampshire local services in 1957 which, in turn, gradually reduced the steam fleet. The condition of steam was starting to deteriorate, owing to staff shortages on the maintenance side and the cleanliness of the locomotives was not up to the usual standards. In the opinion of the author, 1957 was the beginning of the end where steam was concerned on the Southern Region, with the older and more interesting classes disappearing, despite the fact that they were not as efficient as the more modern Standard classes. The end of the 'King Arthurs', 'Lord Nelsons' and 'Schools' came in 1962 and this, except for the Pacifics, was almost the demise of former Southern Railway locomotives. Diesels of the Type 2 D5000 class were on loan to the Eastern Section of the Southern Region to help operate the Kent traffic, whilst final details were worked out to introduce third rail electrification to this area in 1961. In the same year, the first of the Southern Region D6500 Class 33 diesels was introduced, which proved to be a very reliable locomotive and which in 1983 is still going strong. From 1964 onwards all kinds of enthusiast's specials ran over the Southern Region bringing unusual steam locomotive classes not normally seen culminating in the run up to electrification in 1967. Over the last few months, footplate crews became very enthusiastic, and gave the enthusiast some rousing runs, with 100 m.p.h. being attained on several occasions and authority turning a blind eye. By this time, the mechanical conditions of some of the Pacifics was deteriorating rapidly, and must have given the crews a rough ride.

Les Elsey
Bishopstoke
Hants
1983

Acknowledgements

I should like to express my thanks to all my fellow photographers for their kind help and for the loan of their prints for this album. My special thanks go to Ted Fry, a friend and photographer for many years who has helped me in many ways.

Finally I should like to thank my wife, Daphne, whose encouragement and support has helped me to complete this project.

All photographs in this album have been taken by the author unless otherwise credited.

Plate 3:   A 'Merchant Navy' class 4-6-2, No. 35013 *Blue Funnel*, powers the 4.55p.m. Bournemouth West to Waterloo as it heads towards Shawford on 26th June 1956. This train is Eastleigh duty 253, which commenced with the locomotive working a stopping train to Bournemouth, then a Bournemouth to Waterloo service, returning with the Weymouth mail train as far as Southampton Terminus.

Contents

Plate 4 (above): 'The Thanet Belle' headed by 'Battle of Britain' class 4-6-2 No. 34064 *Fighter Command*, leaving Broadstairs. This Pullman train, inaugurated on 31st May 1948, ran between Victoria and Ramsgate, calling at Whitstable, Herne Bay, Margate and Broadstairs after leaving Victoria at 11.30a.m., (Sundays to Fridays). On Saturdays, the train left Victoria at 3.05p.m. The normal formation comprised two first class and eight third class Pullman coaches. This Pullman train was later renamed the 'Kentish Belle' and ran until electrification of the Kent Coast lines in 1959.

Author's Collection

Plate 5 (below): The all Pullman boat train, the 'Golden Arrow' leaves Victoria for Dover on 21st August 1952 behind 'Britannia' class 4-6-2 No. 70004 *William Shakespeare*.

Plate 6 (above): Seen approaching Dover Marine Station, on 17th June 1951, is the 'down' 'Golden Arrow' with 'Merchant Navy' class 4-6-2 No. 35028 *Clan Line* in charge. This engine was still in the blue livery which was only carried by this class on the Southern Region from 1949 to 1952.

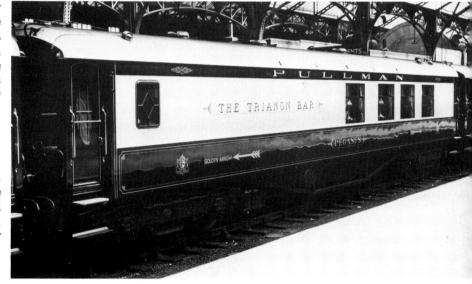

Plate 7 (right): Pullman car *Pegasus*, 'The Trianon Bar' built in 1951, by the Birmingham Carriage & Wagon Co., and part of the 'Golden Arrow' formation, stands in Dover Marine Station after arrival from Victoria.

Plate 8 (right): The 'Golden Arrow' ship *TS Invicta* leaves Dover Harbour bound for Calais where the SNCF 'Golden Arrow' awaited on the quayside prior to leaving for Paris. The *TS Invicta* of 4,191 tons was built in 1940 although ordered before the commencement of World War II, with the intention of operating it on this service. However, it did not take up its intended use until after the war.

Plate 9 (above): An R1 class 0-6-0T, No. 31154 is pictured at Folkestone Junction on 5th May 1951 after banking a boat up the 1 in 30 incline from Folkestone Harbour. A Bulleid Pacific then took the train on to Victoria.

Plate 10 (below): Folkestone Junction Shed, where the bankers were housed for use on the Folkestone Harbour branch. This branch necessitated working three engines, two at one end, and one at the other. For many years, the Stirling R1 class locomotives carried out these duties until they were withdrawn in 1959. They were replaced by Western Region pannier tanks.

London Bridge

Plate 11 (above): A Class 4 Standard 4-6-0, No. 75068 accelerates through London Bridge Station on 14th June 1957 with empty Continental Ferry vans bound for Dover. This train left Ewer Street Continental Depot, situated between Waterloo East and Borough Market Junction, where the vans were unloaded for the London markets.

Plate 12 (below): On 23rd June 1957, a transfer freight from the Eastern Region, bound for a Southern Region marshalling yard, is seen headed by an ex-LNER J50 class 0-6-0T, No. 68920 passing through London Bridge.

Parcels Trains

Plate 13 (left): An ex-SECR Class D 4-4-0, No. 31734 in black lined livery, leaves Ashford on 13th June 1951, with a London bound parcels train.

Plate 14 (right): Simmering away at Bricklayers Arms Shed on 14th April 1951 is ex-SECR Class C 0-6-0 No. 31280. This class of locomotive was the workhorse of the Eastern Section and 109 of these, designed by H. Wainwright, were built between 1900 and 1908.

Plate 15 (right): No. 31086, another ex-SECR Class C 0-6-0, awaits departure from London Bridge with a midday parcels train for Dover on 22nd May 1957. These locomotives were painted in the unlined black livery.

Plate 16 (above): An SECR 0-4-4T, No. 31322 makes a vigorous start away from Ashford with a Margate via Canterbury West train on 2nd June 1951. Set 724 is an ex-LBSCR two car push-pull set and is painted in the BR crimson-lined livery.

Plate 17 (below): Fairburn LMS 2-6-4T No. 42071 prepares to leave Rye with the 6.12p.m. Ashford to Hastings train. These locomotives were built at Brighton in 1951. Of particular interest are the LSWR corridor coaches used on this train.

Plate 18 (above)   A Class W 2-6-4T, No. 31918 hauls a Hither Green to Ashford goods on 6th June 1951 and crosses to the marshalling yard at Ashford from the 'down' local line.

Plate 19 (below)   On a late summer evening, 3 cylinder N1 class 2-6-0, No. 31879 slowly enters Ashford yard with a loaded coal train on 22nd June 1951. There were six of these locomotives in the class, the first, No. 31822, being built in 1923. The remainder of the class, Nos. 31876-80 were built in 1930. Although essentially goods engines with 5ft. 6in. driving wheels, on summer Saturdays prior to the Kent Coast electrification, these engines were used on summer extras to Margate and Ramsgate, and carried out the task with ease.

Plate 20 (above):   The 6.35p.m. Headcorn to Rolvendon train approaches Rolvendon, on 23rd June 1951, behind ex-SECR O1 class 0-6-0 No. 31370 and comprises an ex-LSWR corridor brake.

Plate 21 (below):   On 23rd June 1951, the evening train for Robertsbridge, on the Charing Cross to Hastings main line, is seen leaving Rolvendon and passes the engine and carriage sheds behind ex-LBSCR A1X class 0-6-0T No. 32670 with a SECR 'Birdcage' brake. These engines always worked to Robertsbridge because of bridge weight restrictions on this section. The line closed completely in 1953, the Headcorn to Rolvendon line being taken up almost immediately, but goods traffic on the other section carried on for a while longer. The K&ESR preservation society reopened a half mile section from Rolvendon in 1974, and is gradually extending towards Robertsbridge.

Plate 22 (right): On 15th June 1960, No. 31735, an ex-SECR Class D1 4-4-0, is pictured at Eastleigh Shed. In the last year or two prior to their withdrawal, a few of this class worked on the Western Section.

Plate 23 (right): On 8th June 1951 an ex-SECR Class L 4-4-0, No. 31774, built by Borsig of Berlin in 1914 is seen, carrying the lined black livery and 'British Railways' on the tender, before the lion and wheel emblem was introduced. The locomotive is photographed at Tonbridge Shed.

Plate 24 (right): An L1 class 4-4-0, No. 31786 is seen on Brighton Shed after working a van train on 26th May 1956. Towards the end of its life this class worked from Western Section sheds.

Plate 25 (left): Ex-SECR Class J 0-6-4T No. 31595 was built in 1913. The J class was designed by Wainwright for express work on the Hastings line, but was not successful and only five were built. Only two of the class were finished in the BR lined black livery and all were withdrawn by 1951.

Plate 26 (above): A 'USA' class 0-6-0T locomotive, No. DS238 *Wainwright* is seen, ex-Eastleigh Works, in August 1963 in the lined malachite green livery. Also in the same livery was 'USA' 0-6-0T No. DS237 *Maunsell*, and both locomotives were at Ashford Wagon Works on shunting duties until their withdrawal in April 1967. They are now preserved on the Kent & East Sussex Railway in working order.

Plate 27 (left): On 6th May 1951, ex-SECR Class H 0-4-4T No. 31503, in the lined black livery, is seen on Ashford Shed. This was one of sixty locomotives, built between 1904 and 1915 by Wainwright, being used amongst other duties on push-pull services and carriage workings. This class remained in service until 1964.

Plate 28 (above):   A Newhaven to Victoria boat train crosses Southeram Bridge, near Lewes, on 13th April 1958, headed by 'Schools' class 4-4-0 No. 30910 *Merchant Taylors* and L class 4-4-0 No. 31776. This was possibly a relief boat train as it is composed of ex-LMS stock.

R. C. Riley

Plate 29 (below):   K class 2-6-0 No. 32343, with a summer Saturday through train from the Midlands to Eastbourne, is pictured on 25th July 1953 near Southeram Junction, Lewes.

Plate 30 (right): On 21st July 1953, near Culver Junction, an L class 4-4-0, No. 31780, still in malachite green livery, heads for Lewes with a Victoria to Brighton train.

Plate 31 (above): An ex-LBSCR E4 class 0-6-2T No. 32512 leaves Eridge for Three Bridges with an ex-SECR 'Birdcage' set on 13th July 1953.

Plate 32 (right): On 16th July 1953, ex-SECR D1 class 4-4-0 No. 31727 accelerates away from Lewes and approaches Culver Junction with a Brighton to Victoria via Eridge train.

Plate 33 (left): Heading a push pull train from Brighton to Tunbridge Wells is ex-LBSCR D3 class 0-4-4T No. 32390. The stock is the ex-LBSCR low roofed design, which lasted well into nationalization.

Plate 34 (right): On 13th April 1958, an RCTS enthusiasts' special climbs the 1 in 88 bank to Falmer, between Lewes and Brighton, behind Class 4 Standard 2-6-2T No. 80154, the last engine to be built in Brighton Works, leaving there on 20th March 1957.

Plate 35 (left): A Victoria to Brighton train approaches Lewes, on 17th July 1953, behind Brighton-built Class 4 Fairburn 2-6-4T No. 42105.

Plate 36 (above): Bo-Bo diesel No. 10800 approaches Lewes with a Victoria to Brighton train on 2nd July 1952. This locomotive worked for a short period on the Central Section of the Southern Region, but later returned to the London Midland Region. It was finally broken up in 1976 after being handed over by British Railways to the Brush Group for experimental work.

Plate 37 (right): Co-Co electric locomotive No. CC2 is seen at Barnham on 11th June 1948. This locomotive was painted in the malachite green livery, with British Railways in block shaded lettering, and yellow lines on the cant rail and at floor level.

Plate 38 (left): On 14th July 1953, Co-Co electric No. 20003 heads a goods train east of Lewes. These locomotives mainly hauled the Newhaven boat trains at this time but occasionally were used on goods trains. No. 20003 was painted plain black, with a white band and white numerals.

Plate 39 (above): On 8th June 1957, a Tonbridge via Eridge train leaves Brighton behind a Maunsell rebuild D1 class 4-4-0, No. 31492. This locomotive, rebuilt at Ashford in 1927, was one of the last to be so done. Some others of the class were rebuilt by Beyer Peacock and were quite successful, and smart running was achieved on Kent Coast expresses.

Plate 40 (below): The Eastbourne portion of the Birkenhead to Brighton through train leaves Brighton behind ex-LBSCR Class K 2-6-0 No. 32345 on 27th March 1954.

Plate 41 (above): The RCTS 'Sussex Coast Limited' departs from Brighton on 13th April 1958, bound for Victoria on a 58 minute schedule, behind 'King Arthur' class 4-6-0 No. 30796 *Sir Dodinas le Savage*, one of the batch fitted with six-wheeled tenders for working the Brighton line in the 1930s. The fourth coach from the engine is the twelve-wheeled Pullman buffet car *Myrtle*.

Plate 42 (below): The 11.00a.m. Victoria to Brighton all Pullman train, the 'Brighton Belle', passes Salfords on 30th August 1958. There were three five car Pullman units Nos. 3051-53, two of which were normally used, the third being a spare. Introduced in January 1933, when the Brighton line was electrified, they ran until 1967 when the Pullmans were refurbished and repainted in the standard BR blue and grey livery. The 'Brighton Belle' was withdrawn from service in April 1972 but a number of the Pullman coaches from this train are preserved at various centres throughout the country.   *J. Scrace*

Plate 43 (left): Commonly known as 'Large Vulcans' were the C2X class 0-6-0 locomotives and No. 32437 is seen at Eastleigh Shed on 4th March 1956. There were forty five of this class running in 1948 which were well-liked, except by Western Section men. The last of these was withdrawn in 1962.

Plate 44 (right): H2 class 4-4-2 No. 32424 *Beachy Head* awaits departure from Brighton on 5th October 1952 with the all Pullman train for Victoria celebrating the Brighton Works Centenary. This locomotive was withdrawn in 1958, being the last of the class to go.

Plate 45 (left): An ex-works K class 2-6-0, No. 32353 in the lined black livery and carrying the final lion and wheel emblem is seen at Eastleigh Shed on 1st September 1961. The locomotive is fitted with British Railways AWS gear and the battery box on the footplating should be noted.

Plate 46 (left): Resplendent in lined malachite green livery, at Brighton Shed on 7th May 1948, is ex-LBSCR J2 class 4-6-2T No. 32326. There were two 4-6-2 tank locomotives built by Marsh in 1910 and 1912 with the first, No. 32325 having Stephenson's valve gear, whilst No. 32326 was fitted with Walschaerts. Both engines were withdrawn in 1951.

Plate 47 (right): An ex-LBSCR I1X class 4-4-2T, No. 2002, still in the wartime black Southern livery at Brighton on 19th July 1951. The locomotives were not very successful in their early years but after certain modifications, were relegated to more local duties where they lasted for many years. No. 2002 was withdrawn in 1951 and was the last in the class to go.

Plate 48 (left): No. 32028, an ex-LBSCR I3 class 4-4-2T in the lined black livery, but without any form of identity on the side tanks, is pictured at Eastleigh awaiting scrapping on 23rd September 1951. This locomotive was painted in the early days of nationalization when no decision had been made regarding the insignia to be used. Earle Marsh built twenty seven locomotives between 1907 and 1913 which became instantly successful, working most of the expresses to the coast. The last of the class was withdrawn in 1952.

Plate 49 (above): A local pick-up freight from Eastbourne approaches Southeram Junction, bound for Lewes, on 22nd July 1953, behind ex-LBSCR E5 class 0-6-2T No. 32588. Thirty of these locomotives were built between 1902 and 1904 to the designs of R. Billinton, and the last of the class was withdrawn in 1956.

Plate 50 (below): Ex-LBSCR E4 class 0-6-2T No 32515 shunts in Lewes goods yard on 17th July 1953. This class, also designed by Billinton, was successful on both passenger and goods work, and had only 5ft driving wheels. Seventy five of this class were built between 1897 and 1903, the last of which was withdrawn in 1963. No. 473 *Birch Grove* is preserved on the Bluebell Railway.

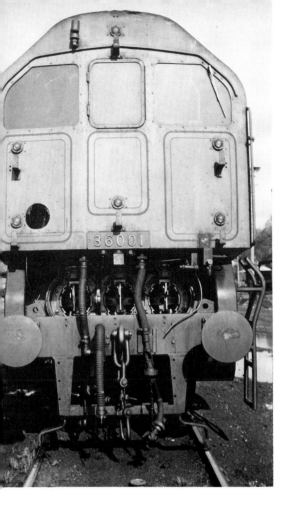

'Leader' Class

Plate 52 (above): No. 36001 crosses to the 'up' main line at Allbrook on a trial run from Eastleigh to Woking on 23rd August 1950. The LNER dynamometer car is next to the locomotive. Several other trial runs were made in the area, and also around Brighton.

Plate 53 (below): Another view of No. 36001, again at Eastleigh, showing the position of the fireman's compartment. The fireman's work on these locomotives was a hot and extremely uncomfortable job and, at Eastleigh, only one crew would volunteer to man this engine. The locomotive was painted silvery grey, with black and dark grey lining. Nos. 36002-4 were partly built but were all withdrawn in 1951.

Plate 51 (above): Bulleid's 'Leader' class 0-6-6-0 No. 36001 is pictured at Eastleigh on 1st October 1950. The cab end shows the front of the bogie and three of the six cylinders with the sleeve valve gear.

Hayling Island Branch

Plate 54 (left): Portcreek Junction on the morning of Sunday, 14th September 1958. An ex-LBSCR A1X class 0-6-0T No. 32650 works the 9.05a.m. Fratton yard to Havant empty coaching stock train, which will form the first train to Hayling Island. The stock is of particular interest comprising a Collett composite brake, an ex-LSWR non-corridor and a standard non-corridor coach.

Plate 55 (above): Ex-LBSCR A1X class 0-6-0T No. 32646 leaves Havant with the 12.05p.m. all stations to Hayling Island train on 19th July 1959. The train is formed of two Bulleid corridor coaches, a BT non-corridor compartment coach and a CCT. The use of the van was mainly for prams, as the guard's van space was inadequate, especially at weekends in the summer when the weather was sunny and traffic became heavy.

Plate 56 (left): The 11.05a.m. Havant to Hayling Island train, hauled by A1X class 0-6-0T No. 32661, crosses the swing bridge over Langstone Harbour on 19th July 1959.

Plate 57 (left): No. 32662, an ex-works A1X class 0-6-0T loco-motive, is seen at Eastleigh on 31st March 1961. These engines were commonly known as 'Rooters' and were well-liked at Fratton Shed although tall fire-men found difficulty in firing them owing to the small cabs. Thirteen engines were rebuilt to A1X class, a number of which are preserved.

Plate 58 (right): An A1X class 0-6-0T, No. 32640 approaches Langstone with a Hayling Island train on 19th July 1959. On this occasion a covered goods van is provided for the prams, which is unusual.

Plate 59 (below): Later the same day, No. 32640 rolls to a halt with the 3.05p.m. Havant to Hayling Island train at North Hayling. A noticeable feature of the class is the different size bunkers, and the spark arresters which were fitted to the chimney because of the fire risk on the wooden swing bridge at Langstone.

Plate 60 (above): A view of Ryde St. Johns Shed on 17th August 1961. Locomotives standing outside the shed are (left to right) ex-LSWR O2 class 0-4-4T No. 31 *Chale*, No. 36 *Carisbrooke* and (front to rear), No. 16 *Ventnor*, No. 14 *Fishbourne* and No. 29 *Alverstone*.

Plate 61 (above): The nameplate of No. 36 *Carisbrooke*.

Plate 62 (right): On 18th May 1952, ex-LSWR O2 class locomotive No. 33 *Bembridge*, is pictured at Newport Shed. This locomotive was formerly No: 218, transferred to the Isle of Wight in May 1936 and withdrawn in December 1966.

Plate 63 (above): An RCTS enthusiasts' special approaches Newport from Cowes, behind ex-LBSCR E1 class 0-6-0T No. 3 *Ryde* on 18th May 1952.

Plate 64 (below): On the same day, a Cowes to Ryde Pier Head train runs into Newport, behind ex-LSWR O2 class 0-4-4T No. 28 *Ashey*. A notable feature is the retaining of the cast oval plate on the bunker. The Cowes to Smallbrook Junction section of the railway closed on 21st February 1966.

Plate 65 (left): No. 32 *Bonchurch*, an O2 class 0-4-4T locomotive, awaits departure, on 18th May 1952, from Freshwater with the RCTS Isle of Wight tour bound for Newport, before travelling to Ventnor West. The Freshwater to Newport section of the railway closed on 21st September 1953.

Plate 66 (right): Another view of O2 class 0-4-4T No. 32 *Bonchurch* showing the lined malachite livery, with Bulleid style lettering. There were twenty three of these locomotives on the Isle of Wight, which were built by Adams from 1889 to 1892 for the LSWR. No. 23 *Totland* was the first to be withdrawn, in August 1955, and the last two survivors were No. 24 *Calbourne* and No. 31 *Chale* being withdrawn in March 1967, the former now preserved at Haven Street.

Plate 67 (right): The nameplate of No. 4 *Wroxall.*

Plate 68 (left): No. 3 *Ryde*, an ex-LBSCR E1 class locomotive, painted black and lettered in the Bulleid shaded style. Designed by Stroudley for the LBSCR in 1881, there were four on the Isle of Wight, Nos. 1-4, which were mainly used for goods duties and shunting on Medina Wharf. At times of pressure they were known to work passenger trains. No. 4 *Wroxall* was the last of the class to be withdrawn, in October 1960.

Plate 69 (right): On the RCTS tour of the Isle of Wight on 18th May 1952, O2 class 0-4-4T No. 14 *Fishbourne* awaits departure from Bembridge for Brading on the line from Ryde to Ventnor.

Plate 70 (right): The last day of steam in the Isle of Wight was 31st December 1966. An O2 class locomotive, No. 22 *Brading* leaves Brading with a Shanklin to Ryde Pier Head train.

Plate 71 (below): On 18th May 1952, O2 class 0-4-4T No. 27 *Merstone* leaves Newport with a Cowes to Sandown train.

Plate 72 (above): No. 31 *Chale* on a crisp winter day, 15th January 1956, between Newchurch and Horringford with a Sandown to Cowes train. The section from Sandown to Newport closed on 6th February 1956.

Plate 73 (below): No. 30 *Shorwell* pulls away from Ryde St. Johns Road, on 18th May 1952, with a Cowes bound train, which leaves the Ventnor line at Smallbrook Junction, passing through the principal town, Newport.

Plate 74 (above): An enthusiasts' special headed by 'N' class 2-6-0 No. 31411 passes, on 20th February 1966, over Fort Brockhurst level crossing on the Gosport to Fareham line. Passenger services ceased over this line on 8th June 1953, but goods traffic is still maintained, to the Royal Naval depot at Bedenham.

C. Elsey

Plate 75 (below): Under a rather stormy looking sky, on 16th July 1961, Class 5 Standard 4-6-0 No. 73116 *Iseult* leaves Fareham, with a Sunday Portsmouth to Cardiff through train, formed of LMS/GWR corridor stock. Locomotive change-over took place at Salisbury.

Plate 76 (above): A Bournemouth to Brighton through train climbs the 1 in 105 bank to Woolston, behind ex-LBSCR H2 class 4-4-2 No. 32425 *Trevose Head* on 21st April 1956. These engines worked this train quite regularly at this time. At weekends the load increased to about seven coaches.

Plate 77 (right): On 6th February 1956, a misty winter morning, a Portsmouth & Southsea to Salisbury semi-fast train, headed by ex-LSWR T9 class 4-4-0 No. 30300, approaches Bitterne.

Plate 78 (right): A through Brighton to Plymouth train, complete with a buffet-restaurant set, loaded to twelve coaches, leaves Southampton Central on 9th May 1953 behind Class 4 Fairburn 2-6-4T No. 42103. Salisbury was the next stop, where the engine was taken off and usually replaced by a Bulleid Pacific.

Plate 79 (above): A warm summer morning on 21st July 1951, as ex-LSWR L12 class 4-4-0 No. 30415 is seen passing Northam Junction, with a train of LSWR 'Ironclads' forming a Portsmouth Harbour to Cardiff through train.

Plate 80 (left): On 10th June 1964, fourteen years later, a similar through train, is shown, composed of maroon liveried standard Mk. I corridor stock headed by Class 4 Standard 2-6-0 No. 76062, The train is passing through St. Denys to join the Waterloo to Bournemouth line. The gantry of signals disappeared in 1981 when colour light signalling was introduced.

Plate 81 (left): With the introduction of the 1965 summer service, through trains between Cardiff and Portsmouth were worked by Swindon Inter-City Class 123 units. A Cardiff bound train is seen leaving Southampton Central on 31st July 1965.

E. W. Fry

Plate 82 (above): A summer Saturday extra with ex-LSWR H15 class 4-6-0 No. 30488 on a Wimbledon to Bournemouth train on 8th August 1953, passes Bevois Park yard and slows for the 15 m.p.h. check round Northam curve.

Plate 83 (below): On 2nd September 1950, 'Schools' class 4-4-0 No. 30929 *Malvern*, still in the lined black livery, eases a Bournemouth West to Waterloo train away from Southampton Central. On summer Saturdays, all London bound trains carried reporting numbers for regulating purposes.

Plate 84 (above): No. 31898, a U1 class 2-6-0, heads the 10.03a.m. Eastleigh to Fratton goods working, near Knowle Halt, between Botley and Fareham, on 9th March 1961. In the latter days of steam, this class of locomotive was rather uncommon on this line. No. 31898 had previously worked e.c.s from Lancing Carriage Works to Eastleigh.

Plate 85 (below): On the same day 'King Arthur' class 4-6-0 No. 30804 *Sir Cador of Cornwall* heads a short van train from Eastleigh to Portsmouth & Southsea, passing Knowle Junction box. The Meon Valley line joins from behind the box. The 'up' and 'down' line from this point to Fareham is now closed and the original line in the foreground is operated as 'reversible' under the present Eastleigh MAS scheme. Knowle box closed when the MAS scheme came into operation.

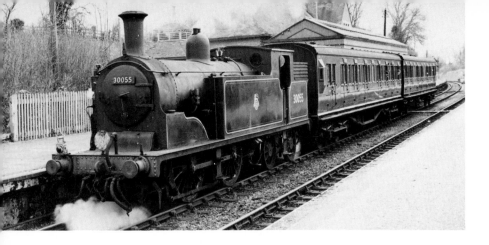

Meon Valley Branch

Plate 86 (left): The Alton to Fareham push-pull train is seen about to leave Droxford pushed by ex-LSWR 0-4-4T No. 30055, on 17th April 1954.

Plate 87 (right): On 17th April 1954, a goods train from Alton to Fareham leaves Wickham behind an ex-LSWR T9 class locomotive, No. 30726, after shunting the yard.

Plate 88 (left): An RCTS special 'The Hampshireman' crosses West Meon Viaduct for the last time on Sunday 6th February 1955, hauled by T9 class locomotives Nos. 30301 and 30732. Scheduled passenger services had ceased the day before. This special also marked the closing to passengers of the Pulborough to Petersfield line.

Plate 89 (right): Ex-LSWR M6 class 0-4-4T No. 30110 is pictured, on 3rd May 1953, emerging from Fareham Tunnel, with a four coach push-pull special from Bishop's Waltham to Havant. This line is the present Fareham to Eastleigh line and was formerly used by Meon Valley trains and those calling at Knowle Halt. The line is now singled as far as Botley.

Bishop's Waltham Branch

Plate 90 (right): An RCTS special on 14th June 1952 awaits departure from Bishop's Waltham for Eastleigh, behind ex-LSWR C14 class 0-4-0T No. 30589 with a push-pull set in the lined crimson livery. The locomotive ran round the train at Botley before departing for Eastleigh. Passenger services ceased on this line in January 1933.

Plate 91 (left): On 26th April 1952, a spring morning, the daily goods from Bishop's Waltham to Eastleigh, hauled by ex-LSWR M7 class 0-4-4T No. 30480, passes near the site of Durley Halt.

Plate 92 (right): The same locomotive has just arrived from Eastleigh at Bishop's Waltham, and is just about to carry out some shunting before returning on 10th May 1952. The site of this yard is now covered by a roundabout on the A32 road.

Plate 93 (above):   An Eastleigh to Fawley goods train accelerates through Southampton Central, behind ex-LSWR H16 class 4-6-2T No. 30516, on 15th October 1960.

Plate 94 (below):   On a summer evening, 6th September 1962, an empty tanker train leaves Eastleigh for Fawley behind W class 2-6-4T No. 31922. This is an empty block train from Bromford Bridge returning to the Esso Refinery. The locomotive is changed at Eastleigh for a tank engine, because of the difficulty in running tender first over ungated crossings on the Fawley branch and the possibility of road traffic accidents.

Fawley Branch

Plate 95 (right): The 12.45p.m. Fawley to Eastleigh (SO) train awaits departure from Fawley, on 4th April 1953, behind Class 3 Standard 2-6-2T No. 82015. The chimney in the background is at the original Agwi Refinery which, opening in 1949, expanded into the present Esso Refinery, covering a far greater area, and sidings for the rail traffic. Passenger services which were sparse and, towards the end, were worked by Hampshire diesel electric multiple units, ceased in February 1966. Since the end of steam, traffic is worked mainly by Class 33 and Class 47 diesels.

Plate 96 (above): A line up of ex-LSWR locomotives at Eastleigh Shed on 29th August 1960. From left to right are T9 class 4-4-0 No. 30707 and H16 class 4-6-2T locomotives Nos. 30518, 30516 and 30520, the latter being ex-works. The H16 class engines had just come to Eastleigh to work the Fawley trains and No. 30516 made several test runs over the branch but after about a year, W class tanks took over after being displaced on London goods turns by diesels. The H16 class was withdrawn in December 1962.

Plate 97 (right): An RCTS special, headed by 'USA' class 0-6-0T No. 30062, from Fawley to Southampton Docks, crosses an ungated roadway near Pooks Green on 17th May 1953.

E. W. Fry

Plate 98 (above): S15 class 4-6-0 No. 30834, fitted with a 4,000 gallon tender, leaves Eastleigh with the 5.22p.m. service to Portsmouth & Southsea. A Hampshire diesel electric multiple unit is seen leaving at the same time with the 5.05p.m. Romsey to Southampton Terminus train.

Plate 99 (below): On a bright frosty morning, 26th December 1956, Doncaster-built Class 4 Standard 2-6-0, No. 76063, passes Eastleigh South Junction, with the 9.10a.m. Reading General to Portsmouth & Southsea train.

Plate 100 (above): During the evening of 16th July 1956, S15 class 4-6-0 No. 30838 'has the road' through Eastleigh with a Southampton Docks to Nine Elms banana train.

Plate 101 (below): An unusual visitor to the area on 17th August 1966 was 'Britannia' class 4-6-2 No. 70004 *William Shakespeare*. It is seen pulling away on the 'up' slow line at Allbrook, with a Southampton Docks to Banbury banana special. This locomotive had arrived on the Southern Region to work an enthusiasts' special the week before, and was also used for other work including boat trains from Waterloo to Southampton Docks.

C. Elsey

Plate 103 (right): A 'West Country' class 4-6-2, No. 34043 *Combe Martin* is seen in ex-works condition on 17th June 1952. Its modifications include wedge-shaped cab and cut down tender, and it carries the lined panel livery on the cab without the black skirt along the cab and tender.

Plate 104 (left): Heading into the setting sun, a return excursion from Portsmouth Harbour to Chippenham approaches Chandler's Ford, on 14th June 1960, behind 'Battle of Britain' class 4-6-2 locomotive, No. 34058 *Lord Beaverbrook*. This section of line between Romsey and Eastleigh is now singled but still carries up to thirty trains a day. This includes stone traffic and one regular passenger train daily Monday to Friday, the 8.57a.m. service from Southampton to Bristol, this being worked by a Class 33 diesel.

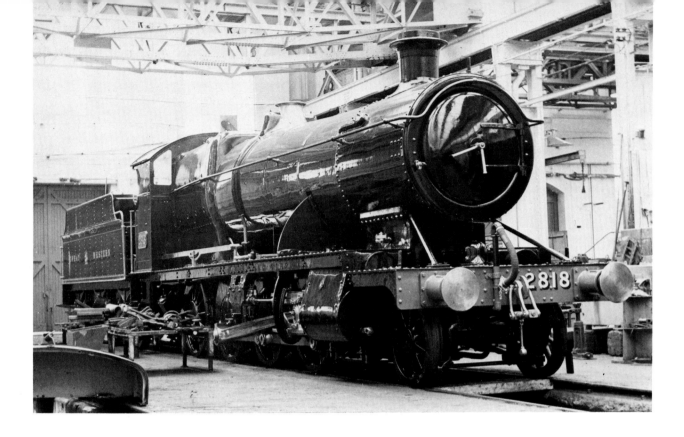

Eastleigh Works

Plate 105 (above): A sight one would never expect to see in Eastleigh Works was that of GWR 2-8-0 No. 2818, looking resplendent after overhaul on 8th April 1967. This locomotive is now in the National Collection at the National Railway Museum, York.

Plate 106 (below): On 26th September 1966, 'Schools' class 4-4-0 No. 926 *Repton* was under restoration, at Eastleigh, to her original Southern Railway condition and olive green livery. This locomotive was shipped, in working order, to Steamtown, USA.

Plate 107 (above): No. 35017 *Belgian Marine*, a 'Merchant Navy' class 4-6-2 locomotive, almost complete after rebuilding, is seen in the erecting shop at Eastleigh Works on 30th March 1957.

E. W. Fry

Plate 108 (below): On 7th November 1959, 'Battle of Britain' class 4-6-2 No. 34049 *Anti-Aircraft Command* is seen undergoing heavy repair in Eastleigh Works.

E. W. Fry

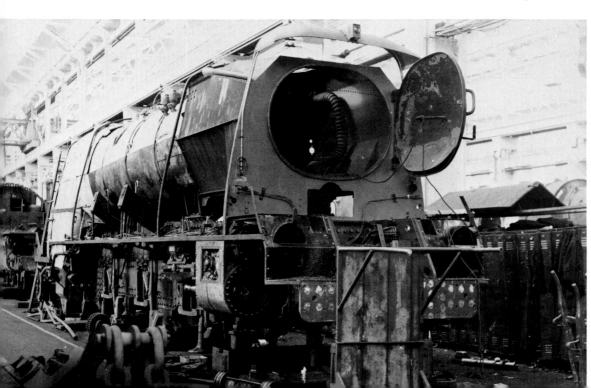

Plate 109 (above): A Ransome & Rapier 36 ton steam crane, No. DS80, from Guildford was on standby at Eastleigh on 10th June 1966 whilst the Eastleigh crane was under overhaul in the works.

Plate 110 (below): Eastleigh Motive Power Depot's coaling stage, where coaling was by four-wheeled tubs. A rotary conveyer belt was also available but it was rarely used. No. 31793, a U class 2-6-0, fitted with British Railways AWS, takes water before being coaled on 10th June 1966.

Plate 111 (above): On 10th June 1962, a rather dirty 'Hall' class 4-6-0, No. 5953 *Dunley Hall*, heads westwards between Eastleigh and Chandler's Ford with a Portsmouth Harbour to Filton excursion train.

Plate 112 (right): On 13th April 1959, empty bogie hopper wagons, bound for Meldon Quarry, thread their way through the cutting near Chandler's Ford behind 'Battle of Britain' class 4-6-2 No. 34049 *Anti-Aircraft Command*.

Plate 113 (left): A sight gone for ever, at least on the Southern Region, is that of loaded cattle wagons in a train next to the locomotive. Ex-LSWR H15 class 4-6-0 No. 30333, with a Eastleigh to Chichester goods, is seen near Botley on 13th October 1956. No. 30333 was withdrawn from service in October 1958.

Plate 114 (above): Climbing the 1 in 161 bank from Halterworth Crossing towards Chandler's Ford, on 26th May 1956, is Class 3 Standard 2-6-2T No. 82015 with the 9.30a.m. Andover Junction to Eastleigh train.

Plate 115 (left): At the same location, on 26th May 1956, H15 class 4-6-0 No. 30476 climbs steadily, with steam to spare, on a Salisbury to Eastleigh goods train.

Plate 116 (left): Ivatt Class 2P 2-6-2T No. 41293, fitted with the tapered chimney for improved steaming, pulls away from Chandler's Ford on, 21st June 1952, with a Romsey to Eastleigh local train.

Plate 117 (right): The daily goods from Longparish to Andover Junction is pictured, near Fullerton Junction, behind ex-LSWR 4-4-0 No. 30289 on 12th June 1954. This branch became very busy in World War II serving RAF establishments, and the siding accommodation at Longparish had to be increased. Afterwards, traffic gradually diminished and the line closed on 28th May 1956.

E. W. Fry

Plate 118 (above): On a misty morning, 10th January 1953, ex-GWR 45XX class 2-6-2T, No. 4538, hurries through Romsey with a goods train from Andover to Southampton. This class of locomotive was not often seen south of Andover Junction.

Plate 119 (right): A lovely spring day in the Test Valley and GWR 'Manor' class 4-6-0, No. 7808, *Cookham Manor* coasts along near Nursling with the Cheltenham to Southampton Terminus (via M&SWJR) train on 17th March 1956. For a long time, this locomotive was a regular visitor to Southampton on this working, and it is now preserved at Didcot.

Waterloo

Plate 120 (right): The 'Atlantic Coast Express', hauled by 4-6-2 'Merchant Navy' class No. 35015 *Rotterdam Lloyd*, in blue livery, awaits departure from Waterloo on 11th June 1951. Next to the engine is the Ilfracombe portion of the train which is formed of several through coaches, except on Saturdays when the 'Atlantic Coast Express' was run in several sections to various destinations in the West of England.

Plate 121 (left): An ex-LSWR M7 class 0-4-4T, No. 30319, is seen at Waterloo after banking a train away from the platform. These locomotives did sterling work for many years on carriage workings to and from the carriage sidings at Clapham Junction, steam heating the trains before the train engines were attached. After World War II, several of the M7 class locomotives at Waterloo were painted in malachite green with the words 'British Railways' on the bunker, but this only lasted until March 1953 after which they were painted in the lined black livery.

Plate 122 (right): On a misty winter day, 29th October 1951, 1,750hp 1Co-Co1 diesel-electric locomotive, No. 10202, awaits departure from Waterloo with the 1.00p.m. Waterloo to Exeter train. This locomotive, along with Nos. 10201, 10000 and 10001, was transferred to the Southern Region to work two round trips daily, six days a week, between Waterloo, Exeter and Weymouth, in addition to the Bournemouth Belle on Sundays.

Plate 123 (above): A 'Merchant Navy' class 4-6-2, No. 35008 *Orient Line* sweeps round the curve under the 'up' Bournemouth line at Worting Junction with the 1.00p.m. Waterloo to Exeter train on 3rd August 1957.

Plate 124 (below): An LCGB enthusiasts' special rounds the curve at Salisbury Tunnel Junction behind 'West Country' class 4-6-2 No. 34006 *Salisbury* on 3rd July 1966. The Southampton line from Salisbury bears away to the right.

C. Else

Bulford Branch

Plate 125 (right): A troop train hauled by 'Battle of Britain' class 4-6-2 No. 34052 *Lord Dowding* and 'West Country' Pacific No. 34047 *Callington*, both later rebuilt, passes the former site of Newton Tony Station. These troop specials required double-heading on the steep inclines on the branch which included gradients of 1 in 60 out of Amesbury and 1 in 165 from Grateley to Bulford.

E. W. Fry

Plate 126 (above): On 14th May 1955, an enthusiasts' special from Andover Junction to Bulford and return is worked by Beattie 0298 class 2-4-0WT No. 30587, with an ex-LSWR three coach non-corridor set, and is seen passing the site of Newton Tony Station. The engine was turned on the turntable at Amesbury, the next station on the return journey.

Plate 127 (right): On 28th June 1952, the last passenger train to Bulford is pictured leaving Salisbury, behind No. 30317, an ex-LSWR 700 class 0-6-0, with two coaches. At this time, the branch was still open for troop specials and for freight to Bulford Camp but closed completely in March 1963.

E. W. Fry

Plate 128 (above): A Cardiff-allocated 'Britannia' class 4-6-2, No. 70027 *Rising Star*, leaves Salisbury with a Portsmouth Harbour to Cardiff through train on 17th June 1953.

E. W. Fry

Plate 129 (below): On the morning of Sunday, 14th January 1963, 'Battle of Britain' class 4-6-2 No. 34052 *Lord Dowding* pulls away from Salisbury Station with a Waterloo train.

Plate 130 (right): No. 31638, U class 2-6-0, prepares to leave Salisbury, on 25th April 1954, with a stopping train for Exeter. Instead of carrying the usual rectangular lining, the 3,500 gallon tender is lined all around the edge.

Plate 131 (above): On 16th September 1950, Z class 0-8-0T No. 30957, for many years stationed at Salisbury, shunts a loaded coal train from South Wales in East yard. When this duty was taken over by 350hp diesel shunters, these engines progressed to the working of the Fawley goods trains and Exeter St. David's banking duties for varying periods until their withdrawal in November 1962.

Plate 132 (right): On 5th August 1957, 'Merchant Navy' class 4-6-2 No. 35009 *Shaw Savill* heads the 4.05p.m. (SO) Exeter to Waterloo train, and rounds the curve prior to braking for the speed restriction at Wilton.

E. W. Fry

'Devon Belle'

Plate 133 (above): The Ilfracombe portion of the 'up' 'Devon Belle' enters Exeter St. David's, on 28th August 1954, behind 'Battle of Britain' class 4-6-2 No. 34058 *Sir Frederick Pile*. The 'Devon Belle' first ran in 1947 in the summer timetable, from Friday to Monday. There were two trains, each of twelve cars, and each with an observation car. The train ran non-stop from Waterloo to Sidmouth Junction and engine changes were carried out in both directions at Wilton, west of Salisbury. The Ilfracombe portion was formed of eight cars including the observation car, with four cars being for Plymouth. After each trip the observation cars were turned round at London and Ilfracombe. In 1949 the Plymouth portion was discontinued and the train was withdrawn after the 1954 summer season.

R. C. Riley

Plate 134 (below): The 'up' 'Devon Belle', headed by 'Merchant Navy' class 4-6-2 No. 35005 *Canadian Pacific*, coasts towards Salisbury for the speed restriction through the station, a locomotive change having been made at Wilton. No. 35005 was fitted with a mechanical stoker from March 1948 until April 1951 but it was removed, as it did not produce the economies desired, and the locomotive was rebuilt in May 1959.

E. W. Fry

Plate 135 (above):   All stations to Exeter Central. On 16th August 1964, Class 4 Standard 2-6-0 No. 76005 leaves Tisbury on a hot summer afternoon.

Plate 136 (below):   A Waterloo to Exeter train, headed by 'Merchant Navy' class 4-6-2 No. 35026 *Lamport & Holt Line*, passes Semley on 16th August 1964. The fourth vehicle from the engine is a Mk. I RKB, one of two, numbered S1552 and S1553, which were allocated to the Southern Region's West of England services.

Plate 137 (above): A 'West Country' class 4-6-2, No. 34002 *Salisbury*, rounds the curve and approaches Semley, after climbing the 1 in 130/100 incline for nearly four miles, with an 'up' West of England express on 16th August 1964.

Plate 138 (below): Class 5 Standard 4-6-0 No. 73171 accelerates downhill, after a steady climb for eight miles to Semley, with the through Brighton to Plymouth train on 16th August 1964.

Plate 139 (right): The 11.00a.m. (SuO) Exeter to Waterloo train passes Milbourne Port, on 2nd September 1962, headed by 'Schools' class 4-4-0 No. 30925 *Cheltenham.* This class of locomotive was rather unusual west of Salisbury and this working, at the end of the summer, was one of the last main line workings of this class. No. 30925 is now preserved at the National Railway Museum, York.

W. M. J. Jackson

Plate 140 (above): A 'King Arthur' class 4-6-0, No. 30456 *Sir Galahad,* with 'British Railways' on the tender, was built in 1925 and withdrawn in May 1960. This class of locomotive spent most of its days working between Salisbury and Exeter until the advent of the Bulleid Pacifics.

Plate 141 (right): A 'Lord Nelson' class 4-6-0, No. 30861 *Lord Anson,* breasts the summit of the 1 in 100 incline between Templecombe and Milbourne Port, on 2nd September 1962, whilst hauling a special from Waterloo to Sidmouth Junction. This class was not often seen west of Salisbury in post-war years.

W. M. J. Jackson

Plate 142 (above): Through coaches detached at Axminster from the 10.45 a.m. ex-Waterloo, thread their way behind ex-LSWR 0415 class 4-4-2 tanks, Nos. 30583 and 30584, between Axminster and Combpyne on 16th July 1960. The branch twists and turns throughout the 6¾ miles, with gradients of 1 in 40/60 to the summit falling at 1 in 82/94 to the terminus at Lyme Regis which is 250ft. above sea level and half a mile from the town centre.

T. Molyneaux

Plate 143 (left): Waiting in the bay at Axminster, on 7th September 1952, is an 0415 class 4-4-2T, No. 30584, being coaled at the coaling stage. The locomotive is in a plain black livery with yellow shaded lettering.

Plate 144 (left): At Lyme Regis, on 7th September 1952, No. 30584 waits to return to Axminster after running round its train. The ex-LSWR two coach set has been rebuilt with standard Southern steel underframes. Partly from through workings, corridor stock is predominant on summer Saturdays.

Plate 145 (right): On 30th July 1961, No. 35010 *Blue Star*, a 'Merchant Navy' class Pacific, shunts the 1.15a.m. (SuO) Salisbury to Yeovil Town train into the sidings. On arrival at Yeovil Junction, this locomotive will be turned on the turntable before proceeding to Yeovil Town. Yeovil Shed is on the right, and in 1967 the whole of the area around the station and shed was razed to the ground, and is now a car-park.

E. W. Fry

Plate 146 (left): No. 30131, an M7 class 0-4-4T, propels its train from Yeovil Town to Yeovil Pen Mill on 30th July 1961. All the lines shown have been removed and the line to Pen Mill is now a footpath. The line from Yeovil Junction to Yeovil Pen Mill is maintained by the wartime connection.

E. W. Fry

Plate 147 (right): On 31st May 1953, a Waterloo to Exeter service leaves Sidmouth Junction behind Britannia class 4-6-2 No. 70017 *Arrow*. This locomotive was on loan to the Southern Region during the temporary withdrawal of the Bulleid Pacifics for ultrasonic testing of the axles, resulting from one fracturing whilst in service.

Plate 148 (left): T9 class 4-4-0 No. 30729 shunts stock from the 7.30a.m. (SO) Waterloo to Ilfracombe train at Exeter Central on 16th July 1960. Passengers are crossing the platform to join the 11.15a.m. to Exmouth in the bay.

T. Molyneaux

Plate 149 (below): N class 2-6-0 locomotive No. 31841 leaves the Southern line from Okehampton, at Cowley Bridge Junction, on 18th June 1957. It is hauling an Engineer's train from Meldon Quarry to the Southern Region. The line coming in from the right is the Western Region's main line from London via Taunton.

E. W. Fry

Plate 150 (left): E1R class 0-6-2T No. 32094 was rebuilt from an E1 class at Brighton Works in 1927, for work in the West Country and was mainly used for banking duties up the 1 in 37 incline between Exeter St. David's and Exeter Central, and on the Halwill to Torrington branch.

Beattie Well Tanks

Plate 151 (left): An 0298 class 2-4-0WT, No. 30586, awaits general works overhaul, at Eastleigh, on 22nd November 1953. There were differences between this particular locomotive and the other two in the class, as No. 30586 had square boxed-in splashers over the driving wheels and these formed a combined sandbox and splasher.

Plate 152 (above): The Beattie tanks returned on 2nd December 1962 to their old haunts, where they used to work the London suburban services. An RCTS/SLS special from Waterloo to Hampton Court left Surbition with six corridor coaches and 210 tons, double-headed, with Nos. 30585 and 30587 in charge.

E. W. Fry

Plate 153 (left): A Wadebridge to Wenfordbridge goods train crosses the road at Dunmere, on 23rd July 1953, behind 0298 class 2-4-0WT No. 30585.

E. W. Fry

North Cornwall

Plate 154 (right): 'Battle of Britain' class 4-6-2 No. 34081 *92 Squadron* heads the 3.30p.m. Ilfracombe to Exeter Central train, on 31st July 1962, and approaches Barnstaple Junction. The line to Torrington is seen to the left of the signal box.

T. Molyneaux

Plate 155 (left): On 2nd August 1962, Class 2 Ivatt 2-6-2T No. 41314 pauses at Bideford with the 3.15p.m. Barnstaple to Torrington train.

T. Molyneaux

Plate 156 (right): A dull summer day, 1st August 1962, and No. 34074, *46 Squadron* a 'Battle of Britain' class 4-6-2, is seen hauling the 4.50p.m. all stations Ilfracombe to Exeter Central train. It is passing Ilfracombe Shed, which although having no shed allocation, still had its turntable in use.

T. Molyneaux

Somerset & Dorset

Plate 157 (above): On 11th October 1954, S&D class 7F 2-8-0 No. 53810, heads a goods train and climbs out of Bath towards Devonshire Tunnel. It is banked by Class 4F 0-6-0 No. 44560.

E. W. Fry

Plate 158 (below): The 6.52a.m. Cleethorpes to Bournemouth West train coasts down the gradient out of Coombe Down Tunnel towards Midford, behind Class 2P 4-4-0 No. 40527 piloting Class 5 Standard 4-6-0 No. 73050.

Plate 159 (left): After nine miles of 1 in 50 gradient have been experienced, except for a short downhill stretch at Shepton Mallet, the fireman takes a well-earned rest. On 16th August 1958, an S&DJR class 7F 2-8-0, No. 53800 accelerates down the hill to Binegar, with the 12.55p.m. Bournemouth West to Bath train.

Plate 160 (below): A special working, on 25th April 1954, hauled, unusually, by two LMS Class 2P 4-4-0 locomotives, No. 40698 piloting No. 40601, almost at the summit at Masbury.

Plate 161 (right): A 'down' 'Pines Express', hauled by LMS Class 4F 0-6-0 No. 44422, piloting 'West Country' class 4-6-2 No. 34040 *Crewkerne*, is seen, on 16th August 1958, almost at Masbury summit after climbing eight miles at an incline of 1 in 50 from Radstock.

Plate 162 (right): In the station yard at Evercreech Junction, S&D class 7F 2-8-0 No. 53808 waits to work an enthusiasts' special to Bath on 30th September 1962.

Plate 163 (right): On 4th September 1954, a rather overcast day, S&D class 7F 2-8-0 No. 53809 pulls away from Masbury Halt towards the summit with the 2.03p.m. Templecombe to Bath train.

Plate 164 (left): An LMS Class 4F 0-6-0, No. 44560, is pictured in charge of an Engineer's train, at Evercreech Junction, on 30th September 1962. No. 44560, originally S&DJR No. 60, was built by Armstrong Whitworth, in 1922, taken into LMS stock with four others in 1930 and renumbered. They were always known on the S&D line as the 'Armstrongs'.

Plate 165 (left): On 30th July 1955, LMS Class 3F 0-6-0 No. 43216 heads the 2.20p.m. train from Highbridge to Templecombe, and it is seen near Wincanton. This engine, built for the S&DJR in 1902, was withdrawn in 1962.

Plate 166 (left): Passing under the Salisbury to Exeter main line, on 27th April 1958, and through the Templecombe Lower Station, is LMS Class 2 2-6-2T No. 41248 with the 4.40p.m. (Sundays only) milk train from Bailey Gate to Templecombe. All trains which came from Bournemouth West that were scheduled to stop at Templecombe, ran to Templecombe No. 2 Junction and reversed into the Upper Station except for the 10p.m. (SO) all stations Bournemouth West to Templecombe Lower Station train, from which passengers took the footpath to the Upper Station exit.

Plate 167 (right): On 21st July 1962, Class 9 Standard 2-10-0 No. 92210, heads the 7.43 a.m. (SO) Bradford to Bournemouth West train, and is seen approaching Horsington.

E. W. Fry

Plate 168 (right): On 21st July 1962, a 'down' 'Pines Express', is seen approaching Horsington, behind LMS Class 2P 4-4-0 No. 40697 and Class 4 Standard 2-6-0 No. 76013. None of the Class 4 Standards were stationed on the S&D but they formed part of workings from Eastleigh.

E. W. Fry

Plate 169 (below): The 9.40a.m. (Saturdays only) Sheffield to Bournemouth West train bursts out of the twin-bore Chilcompton Tunnel behind an LMS Class 2P 4-4-0, No. 40697, piloting LMS Class 5 No. 44697 on 1st August 1953.

E. W. Fry

Plate 170 (left): The 'up' 'Pines Express' climbs the 1 in 50 incline to Winsor Hill Tunnel on 22nd July 1961, and the pilot engine seems to be doing most of the work. No. 40569 an LMS Class 2P 4-4-0, pilots Class 9 Standard 2-10-0 No. 92000.

Plate 171 (below): The rerouted 'Pines Express' shortly after the final closure of the S&D, although the 'Pines Express' ceased to run over the line after 8th September 1962. The train was routed via Southampton and Reading and the headboard was carried for only a short while after the closure. 'Battle of Britain' class 4-6-2 No. 34085 *501 Squadron* passes Eastleigh East box with this train on 12th April 1966.

Plate 172 (right): LNER Class A3 4-6-2 No. 4472 *Flying Scotsman* heads 'The Farnborough Flyer' and is seen approaching Basingstoke on 10th August 1966. It is noticeable that the locomotive is not carrying a number at this time, as No. 4472 normally ran with two eight-wheeled tenders for provision of additional water, with the second tender having the engine number on the side. The two tenders were used in areas where steam engine servicing had been withdrawn. At this time the Southern Region still had working steam, and before returning north, No. 4472 was serviced at Basingstoke.

C. Elsey

Plate 173 (right) LNER Class A3 4-6-2 No. 4472 *Flying Scotsman* is seen on Eastleigh Shed in June 1964, waiting to return to the north with an enthusiasts' special. The locomotive is pictured before it acquired the extra water-carrying tender.

Plate 174 (left): An LNER K4 class 2-6-0 No. 3442 *The Great Marquess* is seen being serviced at Eastleigh coaling stage, on 12th March 1967, after working a special from London (Victoria) to Southampton, via Brighton, Chichester and Fareham. This locomotive was preserved by Lord Garnock and, at the time of writing, is being overhauled on the Severn Valley line.

Plate 175 (above):   On 12th September 1954, the Leeds to Farnborough special, 'The Farnborough Flyer' leaves the line from Reading West and enters Basingstoke headed by GNR Atlantic 4-4-2 No. 251 piloting GCR 'Director' Class D11 4-4-0 No. 62663 *Prince Albert*. The 'Coronation' beaver-tail coach was removed at Basingstoke for turning before the train reversed to go to Farnborough.

Plate 176 (below):   An unusual line-up awaiting coal on Basingstoke Shed on the same day. 'King Arthur' class 4-6-0 No. 30745 *Tintagel* has its smokebox cleaned out and stands in line with GCR 'Director' class 4-4-0 No. 62663 *Prince Albert*, and GNR Atlantic 4-4-2 No. 251. On the right, the 'Coronation' beaver-tail coach has been turned ready for attachment to the special on its return from Farnborough to Leeds later in the day.

Plate 177 (above):   Basingstoke on 11th May 1966, a rather dull morning. Pacific power is plentiful with 'Battle of Britain' class 4-6-2 No. 34066 *Spitfire* on an 'up' goods and 'Britannia' class 4-6-2 No. 70002 *Geoffrey Chaucer*, with nameplates removed, heading a special from Elgin to Portsmouth. The 'Britannia' had worked from Crewe, via Banbury. 'Battle of Britain' class 4-6-2 No. 34102 *Lapford* stands in the station with a Waterloo to Bournemouth train.

R. Cover

Plate 178 (below):   Ex-GWR 2-6-2T No. 6159, with a Moreton sidings to Basingstoke yard goods train, passes through Basingstoke on 25th March 1965.

R. Cover

Plate 179 (above): On a hot summer afternoon, 3rd August 1957, S15 class 4-6-0 No. 30502 approaches Worting Junction with a a Waterloo to Salisbury semi-fast train.

Plate 180 (below): On 3rd August 1957, a 'down' 'Royal Wessex', the 4.35p.m. Waterloo to Weymouth train, headed by 'Merchant Navy' class 4-6-2 No. 35026 *Lamport & Holt Line*, accelerates after a permanent way check at Worting Junction.

Alton Branch

Plate 181 (left): M7 class 0-4-4T No. 30480 hauls a push-pull train from Alton to Southampton, on 8th May 1955, and is seen leaving Medstead & Four Marks, the present terminus of the Mid-Hants Railway. The line from Alton to Winchester Junction closed to all traffic in 1973.

Plate 182 (right): On a misty Sunday morning, 1st May 1966, a diverted Waterloo to Bournemouth train, headed by 'Merchant Navy' class 4-6-2 No. 35008 *Orient Line*, passes through Itchen Abbas on the Alton to Winchester line. The diversion is caused by engineering works on the Basingstoke to Micheldever section.

C. Elsey

Plate 183 (below): The 'Bournemouth Belle', diverted due to main line permanent way work between Ropley and Alresford, on 8th January 1961 is headed by Class U 2-6-0 No. 31628 and 'Merchant Navy' class 4-6-2 No. 35018 *British India Line*. No. 35018 has since returned to the Mid-Hants Railway for restoration to her former glory and should be steaming again, over this same piece of track in the future.

Plate 184 (right): Class 4 Standard 4-6-0 No. 75068 fitted with a double chimney, approaches Micheldever on 2nd August 1961 with the 7.30a.m. Portsmouth & Southsea to Reading General train comprising all GWR corridor stock. This train shunts into the sidings at Winchester City, to allow the 7.20a.m. Bournemouth to Waterloo train to call at Winchester and then run the 67 miles to London, non-stop, in 72 mins.

Plate 185 (above): On the same day, 2nd August 1961, U class 2-6-0 No. 31797 approaches Micheldever with the 7.32a.m. Woking to Southampton Terminus train.

Plate 186 (left): Near Shawford on 22nd August 1953, 'King Arthur' class 4-6-0 No. 30743 *Lyonesse* heads the 6.22a.m. semi-fast Bournemouth Central to Waterloo train.

Plate 187 (right): On 15th June 1957, the daily Eastleigh to Alton goods passes Shawford headed by ex-LSWR 700 class 0-6-0 No. 30326. These engines were built in 1897, the last of the class being withdrawn in December 1962. Although No. 30316 was withdrawn in December 1962, it was employed as a snowplough, along with two others whilst the arctic conditions prevailed in the winter of 1963.

Plate 188 (left): Wishing everybody 'A Happy New Year' on the last day of the old year, 31st December 1955, an ex-LSWR 0395 class 0-6-0, No. 30566, comes rattling through Otterbourne Cutting with the Winchester Chesil to Eastleigh goods.

Plate 189 (right): Quite a lengthy goods train, running tender first, slowly passes through Otterbourne Cutting on 9th June 1962, behind Class 4 Standard 2-6-0 No. 76029 from Winchester Chesil to Eastleigh.

Plate 190 (above): A lovely morning, 15th June 1957, as ex-GWR 'Hall' class 4-6-0 N. 4920 *Dumbleton Hall* passes Shawford with empty LNER stock after working the 9.55p.m. (FO) Sheffield Victoria to Portsmouth Harbour holiday extra. This engine is being preserved, and it is hoped that it will be back in running order by 1985.

Plate 191 (below): On 28th July 1951, a Southampton Terminus to Reading General train is about to leave Eastleigh behind ex-GWR 'Grange' class 4-6-0 No 6802 *Bampton Grange*. The train comprises all ex LSWR non-corridor stock, the first coach being rebuilt on a modern SR underframe. Eastleigh Station had by 1983 changed very little except for the LSWR fire brigade hose cart, by the engine buffer beam, which disappeared many years ago.

Plate 192 (right): On 30th June 1956, a Waterloo to Bournemouth West train passes Allbrook behind 'King Arthur' Class 4-6-0 No. 30738 *King Pellinore*. These Urie 'King Arthurs', built between 1918 and 1923, were numbered 736-755. No. 30738 was the last to be withdrawn, in March 1958.

Plate 193 (left): A 'down' boat train passes Eastleigh, on 6th October 1956, headed by Class 5 Standard 4-6-0 No. 73115. The Pullman car, the sixth vehicle in the train, provided refreshment facilities on the journey from Waterloo to Southampton Docks.

Plate 194 (below): A rather short van train, with an LMS bogie van on the rear passes Eastleigh East box and heads for Southampton Terminus behind S15 class 4-6-0 No. 30508 on 21st July 1951. Nos. 30504-10 lost their Urie tenders when the 'Remembrance' class 4-6-4T locomotives were rebuilt to tender engines in 1935. The Urie tenders were restored and some became available through the withdrawals of other locomotives after 1955.

Plate 195 (above): A rather unusual sight on the Western Divison of the Southern Region. LNER B1 class 4-6-0 No. 61119 passes Allbrook with a return excursion from Portsmouth Harbour to Leyton on 6th May 1959.

Plate 196 (below): A return excursion, on 12th June 1965, from Portsmouth Harbour to Watford, comprising ex-LMS Stanier corridor stock and hauled by 'Battle of Britain' class 4-6-2 No. 34077 *603 Squadron*, is seen north of Eastleigh. In 1965 complete trains of Stanier stock must have been rather rare as most of this stock had been withdrawn by that date.

Plate 197 (right): On 6th June 1954, a damaged 2BIL electric set leaves the 'up' loop line at Allbrook, behind Q class 0-6-0 No. 30543. The train is bound for the sidings at Micheldever for storing, until Eastleigh or Lancing Works could accommodate the unit for repairs.

Plate 198 (right): A lined-out malachite green liveried 'USA' class 0-6-0T, No. 30064, is seen on a trip working from Eastleigh East yard to Eastleigh Works on 7th July 1967, with a train of containers for repair.

C. Elsey

Plate 199 (below): The fireman acknowledges the guard's signal that the train is complete and moving, as the Fawley to Bromford Bridge oil train, which goes via the Didcot, Newbury & Southampton line, pulls out of the 'up' loop line at Allbrook behind Class 9F Standard No. 92231 on 31st March 1962.

Plate 200 (above): A rather lengthy goods train for ex-LSWR T9 class 4-4-0 No. 30283. It is seen leaving Eastleigh, on 23rd March 1957, and is bound for Southampton Docks marshalling yard.

Plate 201 (below): An Eastleigh to Bournemouth goods, via Wimborne, headed by Q1 class 0-6-0 No. 33020 is pictured, between Swaythling and St. Denys on 6th April 1957.

Plate 202 (right): On 5th September 1953, a Lymington Pier to Waterloo train leaves Southampton Central hauled by ex-LSWR D15 class 4-4-0, No. 30465. This was the first summer that this class of locomotive worked the through trains to Lymington Pier, and although they were replaced by U class 2-6-0s during the following year, they were well-liked and some favourable performances were recorded. No. 30465 was the last of the class to be withdrawn, in January 1956.

Plate 203 (above): A rather murky winter day, 1st February 1952, at Swaythling. 'Remembrance' class 4-6-0 No. 32331 *Beattie* pulls away with the 7.32a.m. Woking to Southampton terminus train. The headcode for this train should be one disc, centre smokebox door, right-hand side.

Plate 204 (right): On 10th March 1963, 'The Hampshire Venturer' enthusiasts' special, headed by S15 class 4-6-0 No. 30510, makes a vigorous start from Eastleigh. The next seventeen miles to Litchfield Tunnel, a ruling gradient of 1 in 252, was a good climb.

Plate 205 (above): A 'Schools' class 4-4-0, No. 30923 *Bradfield*, on 7th July 1959, approaches Shawford with the 'up' 'Normandy Express'. This train connected with British Railways' Le Havre to Southampton Docks service. The name, carried by the coaches only, was first introduced in 1952 and ceased when the BR service to Le Havre was withdrawn in 1964.

Plate 206 (below): At the same location, Shawford, o 7th July 1959, the all first class Pullman train, th 'Statesman', the boat train for the flagship, *Unite States*, which plied between New York an Southampton, is seen. The train is headed by 'Lor Nelson' class 4-6-0 No. 30859 *Lord Hood* and th headboard, of standard Southern Region desig superseded the circular one which was introduced i 1952 after the maiden voyage of the *United States*.

Plate 207 (above): On 22nd July 1952, 'The Cunarder' boat train leaves Southampton New Docks, (now Western Docks), making a fine smoke effect behind the doyen of the 'Lord Nelson' class, No. 30850 *Lord Nelson*.

Plate 208 (below): With the second design of headboard 'The Cunarder' approaches the Canute Road entrance to Southampton Old Docks (now Eastern Docks) behind 'West Country' class 4-6-2 No. 34010 *Sidmouth*.

Plate 209 (left): On 1 April 1954, The 'Union Castle Express', headed by 'King Arthur' class 4-6-0 No. 30782 *Sir Brian* passes Chapel Cross, soon after departure from Southampton Docks. In 1958 this train was re-named 'The Springbok'.

Plate 210 (left): A 'Lord Nelson' class 4-6-0, No. 30857 *Lord Howe* prepares to leave Eastleigh Shed for Southampton Docks, to work 'The Cunarder' boat train to London on 25th September 1954.

Plate 211 (left): On 1 August 1955, 'The South American' boat train of the Royal Mail Line *Andes*, which plied between Southampton and Buenos Aires, heads for Waterloo, and is seen near Stoneham being hauled by 'Lord Nelson' class 4-6-0 No. 30857 *Lord Howe*. Most of these boat trains included at least one Pullman car for refreshment facilities. Other boat trains which carried headboards were the 'Holland-America', the 'Greek Line' and the 'Sitmar Line', all related to shipping lines.

Plate 212 (above): 'Merchant Navy' class 4-6-2 No. 35030 *Elder Dempster Lines* passes Millbrook goods yard on 2nd August 1958. The train has only one twelve-wheeled Pullman brake, the rear one being replaced by a chocolate and cream GUV. Millbrook yard is now the Southampton Freightliner Depot. This Pullman train was inaugurated in January 1936 with a short-lived Weymouth portion, the main train destination being Bournemouth West. The train was withdrawn at the commencement of World War II. On reinstatement in November 1946 as an eight to twelve car formation, the train was maintained until its final withdrawal on the electrification of the Bournemouth line in July 1967.

Plate 213 (below): A diesel-powered 'Bournemouth Belle' passes Eastleigh on 1st March 1953 hauled by ex-LMS Co-Co 1,600 hp locomotive No. 10000. During 1953, Nos. 10000, 10001 and 10201-3 worked this train, mainly on Sundays, until they went to the London Midland Region in 1955.

Plate 214 (above): The 11.30a.m. Weymouth to Waterloo train leaves Southampton Central, on 1st March 1952, behind 1Co-Co1 locomotive No. 10202. This was the return service to Waterloo, having left at 5.40a.m. Another return working was the 'Royal Wessex', leaving Waterloo at 4.35pm. The cycle covered approximately twenty two hours each day.

Plate 215 (below): The Royal Train, en route from Truro to Bournemouth on 15th July 1966, conveying HM The Queen and HRH The Duke of Edinburgh, passes Eastleigh after an overnight stop in a quiet siding, headed by 'Warship' class Bo-Bo No. D806 *Cambrian* in maroon livery. The train travelled over the Romsey to Eastleigh line to avoid reversal at Southampton.

C. Elsey

Plate 216 (above): An unusual class to be seen working on the Western Section of the Southern Region was the D1. No. 31735 is seen working an Eastleigh to Southampton Docks goods train through Swaythling on 17th March 1961. This engine, amongst others, was transferred to the Western Section to replace withdrawn class T9 locomotives, but the D1s were not very popular amongst footplate crews.

Plate 217 (below): Due to engineering work being carried out on the main line overnight, one was able to photograph a rather rare sight on 11th March 1956. A 'Lord Nelson' class 4-6-0 No. 30852 *Sir Walter Raleigh* was captured hauling the 11.25p.m. Nine Elms to Southampton Docks goods between Swaythling and St. Denys, as part of Eastleigh duty No. 253 (SO). This engine is fitted with a rebuilt 'Merchant Navy' class chimney.

Plate 219 (below): An ex-LNER V2 class 2-6-2, No. 60917 slowly eases the 3.30p.m. Waterloo to Bournemouth train away from Eastleigh on 16th May 1953. This locomotive was one of another class loaned to the Southern Region during the temporary withdrawal of the Bulleid Pacifics. Others loaned were Class 5 Standards, LMS Black Fives and 'Britannias'. This temporary measure lasted for about two months.

Plate 223 (left): On 14th October 1961, a push-pull train, set No. 384, composed of ex-LSWR 'Ironclads' with an additional SECR ten compartment coach, nears Lymington Junction with the 2.55p.m. Brockenhurst to Lymington Pier train, propelled by Class M7 0-4-4T No. 30130.

Plate 224 (below): On a lovely summer day, 18th July 1959, 'Schools' class 4-4-0 No. 30906 *Sherborne* speeds through Otterbourne Cutting with the 9.42a.m. (SO) Waterloo to Lymington Pier through train.

Plate 225 (left): Class 33 Type 3 Bo-Bo No. D6512 pulls away from Lymington Town Station with the 12.00 Waterloo to Lymington Pier through train on 2nd July 1966. The overall roof on the station and the engine shed to the rear of the train were demolished by the time the branch was electrified in 1967.

C. Elsey

Swanage Branch

Plate 226 (right): An M7 class 0-4-4T No. 30111 gets into its stride as it leaves Corfe Castle with a Swanage to Wareham train on 1st August 1957.

T. Molyneaux

Plate 227 (right): One of the many specials that traversed the branch before its closure, was the LCGB's 'Dorset Coast Express' headed by 'West Country' class 4-6-2 locomotive No. 34023 *Blackmore Vale*, with Class 4 Standard 2-6-0 No. 76026 at the rear. It is seen, on 7th May 1967, between Corfe Castle and Swanage.

C. Elsey

Plate 228 (right): A summer afternoon scene at Swanage. An M7 class 0-4-4T, No. 30111 prepares to leave for Wareham, on 2nd August 1957, with the branch push-pull train. Waiting in the siding is Class 4 Standard 2-6-0 No. 76008 prior to working a through train to Eastleigh, which was a summer Sunday working.

LSWR

Plate 229 (left): An L11 class 4-4-0, No 172, on 16th May 1951, still in Southern wartime black livery and fitted for oil burning at the time of the coal crisis in 1947. This engine, one of fifteen of the class which were converted, was laid aside in late 1948 due to policy changes brought about by the curtailing of fuel imports into the country. All oil burning locomotives were fitted with electric lighting. The steam generator on the left-hand side of the smokebox is of particular interest and the engine is pictured awaiting withdrawal at Eastleigh.

Plate 230 (right): On 9th April 1955, Urie 'King Arthur' class 4-6-0 No. 30748 *Vivien* is seen in ex-works condition. This engine was converted for oil burning in September 1947 and reverted to coal burning in November 1948 retaining the electric lighting. The steam generator is hidden behind the left-hand smoke deflector. Four other locomotives in the class were also converted; Nos. 30740/45/49 and 52, and No. 30748 was withdrawn in September 1957.

Plate 231 (right): H15 class 4-6-0, No. 30334 is seen on Eastleigh Shed on 1st September 1953. This class of locomotive was built by Dugald Drummond as a four cylinder 4-6-0 in 1906. Nos. 30330-34 were rebuilt by Urie as a two cylinder class, in 1924/25, and were fitted with squat stovepipe chimneys but retained the Drummond tenders of 4,300 gallon water capacity. The class spent most of its life at Salisbury, where crews seemed to get the best out of them, both on passenger and goods workings. In June 1958 No. 30334 was withdrawn.

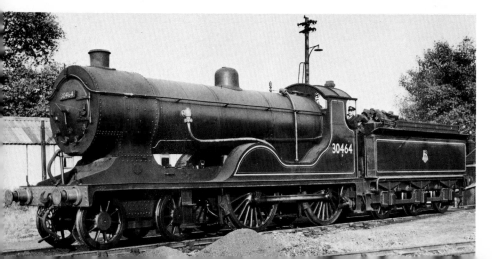

Plate 232 (left): Urie D15 class 4-4-0 No. 30464 stands at Eastleigh on 27th May 1953. These engines did fine work on the main lines of the Western Section of the Southern Region and were well-liked. One of the class, No. 30463, was fitted for oil burning but was scrapped when oil burning ceased in 1948. No. 30464 was withdrawn in September 1954.

Plate 233 (right): Drummond T9 class 4-4-0 No. 30727 is pictured, on 16th April 1955, at Eastleigh, complete with narrow cab, coupling rod splashers and eight-wheeled tender. No. 30120, preserved by the National Railway Museum, York is at present on loan to the Mid-Hants Railway, and is similar to this engine seen in the lined black livery. Other members of the class were fitted with wider cabs, six-wheeled tenders and no coupling rod splashers. The tenders alternated with all members of the class at various times. *(see Plate 77).*

Plate 234 (left): An Adams O2 class 0-4-4T, No. 30229, fitted with a Drummond boiler, is seen at Eastleigh on 27th January 1951. These boilers were poor steamers although this particular locomotive retained it until its withdrawal in March 1961.

Plate 235 (left): Surrounded by snow, No. 30688, a Drummond 700 class 0-6-0, is pictured on 31st January 1954 in ex-works condition. This engine was the first of the class to be withdrawn, in September 1957, after a head-on collision with an electric multiple unit at Staines Central.

Plate 236 (right): Seen at Eastleigh on 14th August 1955, No. 30162, an Adams G6 class 0-6-0T, was the last of the class to be fitted with a vacuum brake, forty seven years after being built in 1900. No. 30162 was withdrawn in March 1958 and another of the class ended up as a Scunthorpe Steelworks shunter from 1949 to 1958.

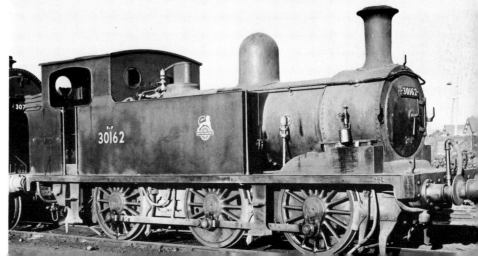

Plate 237 (above): The last scheduled steam passenger working on Southern metals was on Sunday 9th July 1967. The 2.07p.m. Weymouth to Waterloo train, headed by 'Merchant Navy' class 4-6-2 No. 35030 *Elder Dempster Lines*, is seen passing Micheldever. The dates chalked on the smokebox door are incorrect!

C. Elsey

Plate 238 (below): The last days of steam on th Southern Region. A typical scene in the last year steam with locomotives leaving Eastleigh for th scrap-yard. 'Warship' class Bo-Bo No. D846 *Steadfa* is seen towing 'Battle of Britain' class 4-6-2 No. 3408 *615 Squadron* and N class 2-6-0 No. 31411.

C. Els